-ow as in cow

Amanda Rondeau

Consulting Editor Monica Marx, M.A./Reading Specialist

Published by SandCastle™, an imprint of ABDO Publishing Company, 4940 Viking Drive, Edina, Minnesota 55435.

Printed in the United States.

Credits
Edited by: Pam Price
Curriculum Coordinator: Nancy Tuminelly
Cover and Interior Design and Production: Mighty Media
Photo Credits: Brand X Pictures, Corbis Images, Kelly Doudna, Hemera, PhotoDisc, Stockbyte

Library of Congress Cataloging-in-Publication Data

Rondeau, Amanda, 1974-
    -Ow as in cow / Amanda Rondeau.
      p. cm. -- (Word families. Set V)
    Summary: Introduces, in brief text and illustrations, the use of the letter combination "ow" in such words as "cow," "meow," "eyebrow," and "plow."
    ISBN 1-59197-254-X
    1. Readers (Primary) [1. Vocabulary. 2. Reading.] I. Title.

PE1119 .R699 2003
428.1--dc21
                                                  2002038225

SandCastle™ books are created by a professional team of educators, reading specialists, and content developers around five essential components that include phonemic awareness, phonics, vocabulary, text comprehension, and fluency. All books are written, reviewed, and leveled for guided reading, early intervention reading, and Accelerated Reader® programs and designed for use in shared, guided, and independent reading and writing activities to support a balanced approach to literacy instruction.

Let Us Know

After reading the book, SandCastle would like you to tell us your stories about reading. What is your favorite page? Was there something hard that you needed help with? Share the ups and downs of learning to read. We want to hear from you! To get posted on the ABDO Publishing Company Web site, send us e-mail at:

sandcastle@abdopub.com

SandCastle Level: Transitional

-ow Words

chow

cow

how

meow

plow

sow

Mary gave Fluffy some
cat chow.

Amy likes to pet the
baby cow.

Jane is learning how
to ride her bike.

Dave likes to hear his cat meow.

A plow clears the street
after it snows.

The sow is in her stall.

The Sow and The Cow Eat Their Chow

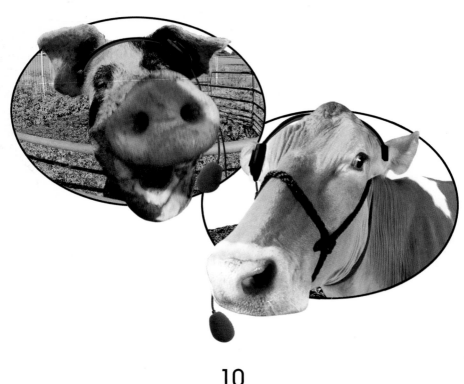

"Hey there, Cow.
Do you see it raining now?"

"Shh!" said the cow
to the pink and black sow.

"Do you hear
the farmer now?"

"No," said the sow.
"I only hear the cat's meow."

"Well," said the cow,
"I wish it were time
for dinner anyhow."

"I made a vow, Sow,
that I would get thinner now."

"But I am hungry and must somehow find chow."

"You must eat now,"
said the sow, "for you are
the farmer's favorite cow."

"I made a vow,"
said the cow,
"but let's eat anyhow!"

So they ate all their chow

and were a happy
sow and cow.

The -ow Word Family

anyhow	now
bow	plow
chow	pow
cow	somehow
eyebrow	sow
how	vow
meow	wow

Glossary

Some of the words in this list may have more than one meaning. The meaning listed here reflects the way the word is used in the book.

chow   slang for food

dinner   the main meal of the day eaten at noon or in the evening

farmer   a person who raises animals, grows food, or both

plow   a machine used to push snow off of streets and sidewalks

rain   water drops that fall from clouds

thinner   more lean or slender

About SandCastle™

A professional team of educators, reading specialists, and content developers created the SandCastle™ series to support young readers as they develop reading skills and strategies and increase their general knowledge. The SandCastle™ series has four levels that correspond to early literacy development in young children. The levels are provided to help teachers and parents select the appropriate books for young readers.

Emerging Readers
(no flags)

Beginning Readers
(1 flag)

Transitional Readers
(2 flags)

Fluent Readers
(3 flags)

These levels are meant only as a guide. All levels are subject to change.

To see a complete list of SandCastle™ books and other nonfiction titles from ABDO Publishing Company, visit **www.abdopub.com** or contact us at:

4940 Viking Drive, Edina, Minnesota 55435 • 1-800-800-1312 • fax: 1-952-831-1632